Cheers
Ray Alan

THE LORD CHARLES WINE GUIDE

Maps by Keith Ratling
Design: Amanda Barlow

ISBN 0 946326 84 3

Typeset by Hourds Typographica
Printed in Great Britain by
MacLehose and Partners,
Portsmouth, Hampshire

Pagoda Books
79 Great Titchfield Street, London W1P 7FN

My sincere thanks to all the distillers and breweries who gave me samples of their produce, thereby making the task of compiling this book very much more pleasurable.

Lord Charles

THE LORD CHARLES WINE GUIDE

PAGODA

FOREWORD

When I heard that my dear old friend had agreed to write this book, I was delighted. I can't think of anyone better than Lord Charles to share his vast experience of alcoholic beverages. For many years, I have been privileged to be his companion: and during this time, I have seldom known him to be completely sober. It was, therefore, only natural that he, above all people, should lend his expert opinion to this subject.

May I wish you, and him, every success: you, as you read and learn; and him, as he spends the royalties on replenishing his wine cellar.

Ray Alan

CONTENTS

INTRODUCTION

A good wine is like a good woman: marvellous to be with, great fun to sample, and to be taken seriously. That's why I don't hold by the practices of those who call themselves wine-tasters, yet insist on spitting the stuff out. I am strongly against this silly habit, and suggest you avoid following this ancient ritual, too. Wine is made for drinking.

Generally speaking, there are three types of wine: cheap, expensive, and damned expensive. But whatever the price, wine is a very personal thing. If you like it, and it suits your pocket, fine. (I don't recommend keeping it in your pocket, but that's up to you.)

I am often asked why it is not done to mix the grape and the grain. In other words, why are we told that mixing wine with spirits is not correct? I often start the evening with a glass of whiskey, followed by a bottle of Soave, and end up with a good brandy, under the table. Indeed, I have met some of my dearest friends there.

Of course, there are some people who insist that such a mix will give you a hangover. Well, I have found the perfect way to avoid this, and I pass the secret on to you with best wishes. Never stop drinking long enough to get one.

Lord Charles

When it came to writing about wine, I did what almost everybody does – faked it.

Art Buchwald

THE ETIQUETTE OF WINE

CELLARING AND LAYING DOWN

Most cellars are cool and made of brick or stone. The best ones are usually underground, which is why the steps leading to them go down, rather than up. It was the Romans who cunningly worked that out, and the idea has never been improved upon.

Laying down is a position with which I am most familiar: but when laying down wine, *you* should be standing up. This makes it easier to place the bottles in the upper racks, unless you have a low cellar. In this case, you can do it from the crouching position. If you don't have a cellar, hard luck.

Red wines should always be placed so that the wine tilts slightly towards the neck of the bottle. This keeps the cork moist and prevents it from shrinking. If air does get in, I suggest you use that particular wine on your fish and chips, or to polish the piano.

It is not generally known that wine reacts to noise and light. So if it's too light in your cellar, I suggest you get the roof fixed, as wine hates sunlight. If you

live near a bus stop, you may find that the noise and vibrations cause your wine to go off slightly. This is because wine doesn't travel well. A cellar away from the bus stop is just the ticket.

It is important to remember that very good, expensive wines are much better off in a glass than a cellar. Always test your wine from time to time. I find that a quick sample four times a day does you and your wine the world of good. And should your cellar have water seeping through it, a good pair of fisherman's waders will come in handy.

So, to sum up, keep your wine in the horizontal position, and it will do the same for you. Make sure the cellar is as dark as possible, especially when showing a lady guest what you've got, whether red or white. The same goes for champagne, unless you happen to live near a bus stop.

SERVING WINE

There is probably more nonsense talked about this than in the House of Lords at Christmas. To serve wine correctly, you require just three things: a bottle, a glass, and a steady hand – unless you don't care about stains on the carpet.

Make sure that your corkscrew is in working order. There is nothing worse than a cork that has crumbled, leaving you with no choice other than to push it into the bottle. This is not only messy, it wastes wine which could otherwise be enjoyed.

Once the bottle is open, place it on one side, and open another which should be of a different colour.

Pour some white into a glass, and twist the bottle slightly as you finish pouring. This prevents that dribble of wine running down the glass into your lap.

When you have finished the white, give the red a good old pour. You must always allow the red to breathe for a while: and it's a good idea if *you* do the same now and then.

Some people like to decant their wine. This is normally done with an oldish wine that has sediment at the bottom of the bottle. I personally prefer to pour straight from the bottle; better still to drink from it.

There are some so-called experts who insist that *all* old wines should be decanted; but I've always held that if a wine is that good, it shouldn't be allowed to get old.

Temperature is another thing that buffs often go on about. White wine should be served chilled, of course; but, then, any fool knows that. Red *must* be served at room temperature, they say. That is all very well if you live in a room that is pleasant and warm. But what if you live in an igloo? If you do, simply place the bottle of red wine in a bucket of hot water. But make sure you have an umbrella handy, as the steam will cause the ceiling to drip.

Champagne and sparkling wines are opened by holding the cork and twisting the bottle, which should be held at an angle of 45 degrees. Never do what those buffoons at office parties do. I refer to pressing the cork out with your thumb, so that the damned thing pops out, bounces round the room, and finally thumps some poor devil in the face. If you see anyone about to do this, take the bottle from him and tell him to shove off. If he won't part with the bottle, then *you* shove off. It's much safer . . . and I should know. I used to be a buffoon.

WHICH WINE WITH WHICH FOOD?

I am often asked this question; so often, in fact, that it's becoming a nuisance. Just drink any wine you fancy with whatever food you desire. It's *your* stomach.

But if you insist, here is a brief guide.

Soup

I suggest a dry sherry. Make it a large, dry sherry. Come to that, why not make it a *very* large dry sherry, and throw away the soup.

Hors d'oeuvres

If you only take a small portion, to tickle the taste buds, I suggest you might try a fruity white. If, on the other hand, you are a greedy devil and insist on piling the plate to overflowing, I suggest a large glass of Alka-Seltzer.

Melon

Here I would suggest a good port. Hawaii or New Orleans spring to mind. But there is always reliable old Ruby. (God bless her.)

Fish

Salmon

I would recommend a bottle of Alaskan white. Not only is it crisp and medium dry, it's very cheap.

Oysters

I recommend champagne. But then I usually do. If you don't have any champers, why not try a bottle of Mombasa Chablis? Poured over the oyster before it is removed from the shell, you can rely on it to kill off any sea fungi that may have grown.

Fish fingers

Here, one has to be careful to choose just the right wine, or you could lose the flavour of the breadcrumbs. A Chateau Poverti would be fine, unless you are covering the dish with tomato ketchup.

Meat

Beef

Generally speaking, red wines seem to be the most popular to serve with beef, unless you don't like them. In this case, you may prefer a white wine.

Lamb

Whether you are enjoying a roast, cutlets or chops, there is only one wine I would thoroughly and heartily recommend. Unfortunately, its name has completely slipped my mind: but if I remember it before the end of this book, I shall certainly give it to you. (It has a white label with gold lettering.)

Hamburgers

This American creation has fast become a favourite all around the world. Even the Russians seem to like them. So what better to go with a beefburger than a young red?

Desserts

I would suggest you give them a miss, and move swiftly to a fine brandy. After two or three, you may find that the coffee has gone cold. Not to worry: it would have kept you awake, anyway, the chances are.

A good general rule is to state that the bouquet is better than the taste, and vice versa.

Stephen Potter, *One-upmanship*, 1952

WINES OF THE WORLD

FRANCE

The French are famous for two things above all others and one of them is making wines. Here are some you may like to try and that even the French themselves are not too familiar with.

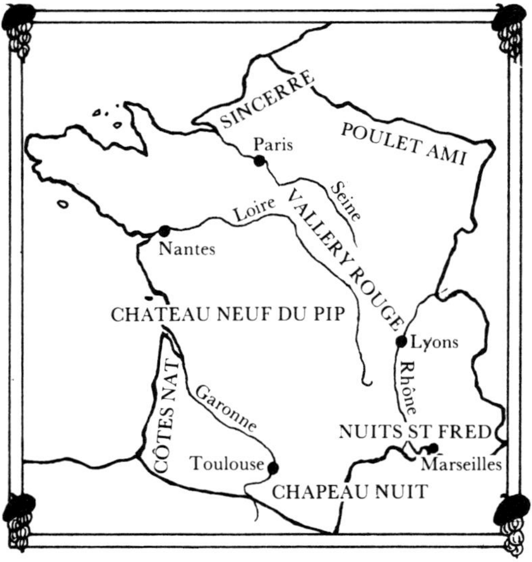

White

Chateau Cerf-Volant

Although it travels well, I find it inclined to cause one to feel high as a kite after just a few glasses.

Chateau Enfants

A very fine young wine, with a character

all of its own. Just the thing for a picnic on the beach, it can keep you happy for hours, then suddenly tire you, and give you a restless night.

Chateau La Peuf

A gay little wine.

Chateau Oignons

Too strong for me. Inclined to burn the throat and make your eyes water, instead of the mouth.

Masquerade La Con

Don't be fooled by this sweet little wine from the Burgundy Valley. It is very dry indeed, and the only thing in its favour is that it makes you thirsty enough to open a bottle of something better.

Saint Point

Created by Madame Point, the famous spiritualist, in 1784. Definitely a medium wine.

Sincerre

A jolly good, straightforward wine with an excellent bouquet. Always reliable.

Villa Dandé Leon

This is a disappointing wine from the Les Champs region. It has a strange yellowish colour, and no bouquet at all.

Villa de la Reine

A rather fruity wine, popular in places, but not the places I go to.

Vin du Fin

This is supposed to be a new wine from the Choufleur vineyard, and it is recommended as a truly excellent accompaniment for a starter. Having tasted it for myself, I can assure you it is definitely the end.

Red

Chapeau Nuit

Often thought of as a perfect night-cap, but too much of the old Chapeau could, in fact, go to your head.

Chateau Le Pied

This comes from one of the few vineyards that still tread the grape by foot, which could account for its remarkable bouquet.

Chateau Neuf du Pip

Made from a large red, fruity grape, here is a good one for wine-tasters to spit out. The pips stick in your teeth and cause great discomfort. If you wear dentures, it can be sheer hell.

Côtes Nat

Guaranteed to keep you warm on those cold winter nights.

Nuits St Fred

If it wasn't French, I'd swear it was made in an old garage, somewhere in Naples. Not to be consumed, but wonderful for getting the car started on a cold morning.

Poulet Ami

This is a truly friendly wine, as the name suggests. The chicken flavour is hardly noticeable.

Rouge du Fard

Here is a good clean red that will really put the colour back into your cheeks.

Vallery Rouge

One of the best red wines to avoid, it is over-produced, over-publicized and over-priced.

GERMANY

Liebfraumilch, Riesling, Sekt and Niersteiner: these are probably familiar names to you. But my researches reveal many other lesser-known German wines you may like to try, and perhaps even lay down, as I often do.

White

Grossefrau
Here is a wine with a much fuller body than most.

Liebfraukrihm
Very similar to Liebfraumilch.

Peasporter

Only drink this from a china mug. A glass allows you to see what you're drinking; and if you could, I assure you that you wouldn't.

Pikkarosen

Here is one of my favourite German whites. I enjoy it in the garden on a summer's evening. Come to think of it, I like it anywhere, any time.

Red Priest

A poor imitation of Blue Nun, it is quite cheap and so could be worth laying down. A dear friend of mine tried some once, and did. (Actually, he *fell* down.)

Rosenkohl

Here is a very unusual German wine. The grape comes from Brussels.

Von Rosenslosh

Here is a wine, far too popular with the vineyard workers ever to get old enough to have a vintage. From the Rosenberg Valley, it can be drunk at any time. And so can you.

Der Schofer

This one could drive you mad, as it is only obtainable at the Karlstadt Garage in Hamburg.

Von Trapp
A pleasant hock, named after the creator of this grape, Hans Offavit. They did call the wine Offavit at first, until a circus act of the same name took them to court, and won.

Red

Bitteschloss
Not a good wine for getting sloshed on. Unlike the Von Trapp, it is too bitter. I understand that the 1998 vintage is going to be less bitter and much better.

Booger Hofgelt
If you want to see your money disappear, this is the wine for you. Most experts agree that it is over-priced.

Ellen-Bogen
Originally from Gilly-Gilly Ossenfeffer, near Katsen. Could be worse, but not much.

Farsteiner
Not to be confused with Niersteiner, it has quite a different flavour.

Federwein
A bottle of this light wine may prove rather heavy on the stomach, but quite pleasant *in* it.

Gropenwein

This one can really get a hold on you. Popular with wrestlers all over the world.

Gutfahrt

The bouquet will often vary.

Liebfahrt

This travels very well, and can be great fun at a party. Have a few glasses and watch your guests change their facial expressions to the 'it wasn't me' look.

Nikkerzoff

A provocative and exciting wine. Very popular with male students at end of term celebrations. Comes from the Unterkleider region.

Rotwein Schlag

Having tasted this, I can only suggest that the vineyard owners be taken to *their* cellars and put down.

Von Klapp

Once you have fallen for this one, you're bound to take more care in the future.

Wunderwein

The only wonder about the famous 'Wonder-wine' from the lower region of the Munich Valley is why they bother.

SPAIN

In addition to Rioja, the Spanish are famous for their Huelva, which is from the Cadiz region. Unfortunately, the best of this wine is not for sale, as it is sent to Jerez for blending. This has prompted me to list a few that no one would ever dream of blending.

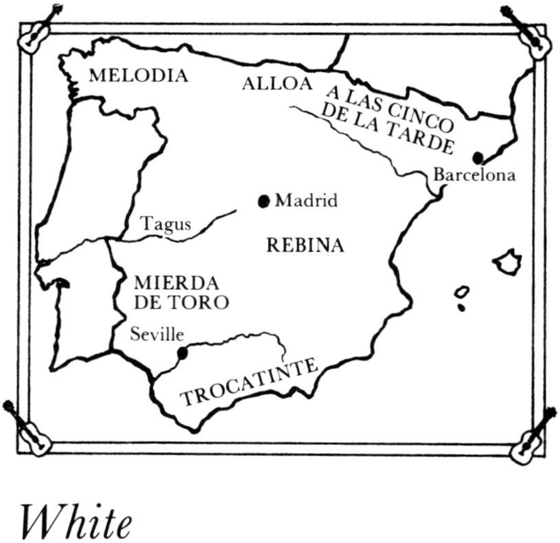

White

A Las Cinco de la Tarde

A small village on the outskirts of Lopez produces several bottles of this wine each week. Ideally, it should be drunk at five o'clock in the afternoon.

Alloa

You would be better off saying goodbye to this. It has the bouquet of a rather cheap air freshener. The 1974 vintage is particularly bad.

Blanco Espumosissimo

This sparkling wine usually gets right up my nose.

Bodega Bonita

I have drunk better. In fact, to be honest with you, I would suggest that, in order to enjoy the unusual bouquet, you would be better drunk.

Mierda de Toro

If a Spaniard tells you that this is a good wine, don't believe him. He's talking a load of mierda de toro.

Rebina Dulce

An el cheapo version of *Rebina Seco*, only it is dry.

Rebina Secca

This can only be described as rather twees and santy. It comes from a dyslexic family vineyard near Madrid.

Vino Condenado

I recommend putting this away under lock and key. Kept for a few years, it seems to improve slightly. You will notice the difference when you take it out, unless you have never had it before.

Vino Dolor de Cabeza

Don't even bother to pull the cork. You are likely to get a terrible headache.

Vino Magico

Pull the cork, and you will be amazed how quickly the wine will disappear.

Vino Venenoso

I don't recommend you to drink this unless you have a doctor nearby. It could be fatal and put paid to all your tax problems.

Red

Carlos Cheste

This one is very good indeed. If you suffer from any bronchial trouble, just rub some on your vest and inhale the powerful fumes.

De Quemar

Not the best red wine in the world, but excellent for cleaning greasy film off the car windscreen. It is also very good for polishing patent leather shoes, so I am informed.

Espantoso

Once described by Columbus as the only thing Spanish worth taking on a voyage. What nonsense! What about Lucilia

Crumpoli, the twenty-two year old Spanish belly dancer? Better than the revolting De Quemar any day . . . and any night, now I come to think of it.

Melodia

This one brings music to my ears, but doesn't do my stomach much good. A bottle is normally followed by some powerful belching.

Trocatinte

This could be nice, if only it were different. The last bottle I tried had a rubbery bouquet which appears to increase as the bottle empties. I think something may have dropped into the vat by accident. I do hope so. I would hate the whole shipment to taste as foul.

Vino Superior

This may look as if it could be a good wine, but it's really very bad. I don't know why they bother to pick the grapes in the first place. (Could we get them under the trades description act?)

ITALY

Valpolicella, Soave, Verdicchio: some of the finest wines come from Italy, which is surprising because the fact that the nation has small feet makes grape-treading tedious. Here are just a few of my recommendations.

White

Barrello

The formula for this wine was stolen from the vineyard of Marco Polo, soon after he invented the game. He used to ride his horses very near the vat, and squash the grapes with his polo stick.

Bella Borsa 1972

Not as good as the previous year's vintage, but there is none of that left, and it is certainly very much better than the year before that. There *is* a lot of that left.

Bella Sophia

If I had to score (and I hope I will before the night is out), I would give this product 11 out of 10. Can't think of anything I enjoy more.

Cornetto Classico

A confident wine that is certainly full of itself. Last week, I was full of it, too: but, amazingly enough, I didn't hurt myself despite falling down all those stairs.

La Mafia Classica

To call a wine after the Mafia may be asking for trouble: and so is your stomach, if you drink it. I hear that they shot the fellow who started it all: serves him right, I'd say.

Luminoso

It's easy to get lit up with this saucy little wine from the Rozzano Bratzi vineyard just north of a town I can never remember. (I probably would have remembered, but I've had rather a lot of the Mafia Classica.)

Piccolo Disco

This is a wine that makes you want to get up and dance. It does at first, anyway. After the fourth bottle, you may find it makes you want to sit down

Pizza Ova

Careful how you call this out to a passing waiter.

Ruffolini

From the suburbs of Florence, this is an aggressive wine which, after one swallow, attacks the lower regions of the oesophagus. Definitely one to avoid.

Tardi Treno

Some wines are so awful that there are no words to describe how sharp-tasting they are. This is one of them.

Terrible

Don't be put off by the name. The taste will do that for you.

Vecchia Pelle

Strange to call a wine 'old leather', you may think: but I am informed that it was created by three hundred shoe-makers in Venice. I am not certain that the story is true, however. Three hundred shoe-makers does sound like rather a lot of cobblers to me.

Vino Odoroso

I should keep well away from this, if I were you. It can be very embarrassing on a crowded train.

Red

Bella Maria

I'm sure she was. But the wine isn't. If you are thinking of something to send to someone you don't like that much, this is certainly it.

Casa Disgustosa

Despite the unattractive name, this really is revolting.

Colli Vino

For a wine that sounds something like a large, hairy dog, it is wonderful value at only 2,000 lire a case.

Due Uvas

Very weak and tasteless, possibly because it is made from only two grapes.

Grande Vino

You get slightly more in these bottles.

Rosso Basso

This is unlike Chianti, mainly because the bottle is a different shape. Apart from that, the colour's the same.

PORTUGAL

The Portuguese are very loyal when it comes to their wines, and hardly ever drink anything that is imported. One of their most successful exports is Mateus. Their Vinho Verde is also popular overseas, possibly because the name is easier to say after you have had a few glasses. Here are some others you can try saying.

White

Puerto Madeira

Despite its name, this Madeira is not a port. It is a light, refreshing white wine, that is ideal with a fish dish. Tests prove that nine out of ten fish prefer it.

Quinta Basto

No worries about which bottle to open with this wine. It only comes in boxes.

Verde Tinto

This beautiful wine is produced on the Algarve coast which can be visited during the summer months.

Red

Basta Quinta

Apart from the old tradition of putting the red Basto Quinta into a green bottle and the white into a brown bottle, this is an uncomplicated wine that you are bound to enjoy, once you have got the hang of which colour bottle to open first.

Vinho Cama

From the Rampanto vineyard near Lisbon, this is a *must* at the end of a wedding feast.

GREECE

You would expect that a land so full of sunshine and antiquities would produce some very varied and satisfying wines, and of course it does. Take Retsina or Kokkineli, for instance. And if you don't wish to take *them*, try one or two of these that I discovered on my recent visit to this delightful country.

White

Kriti Blankos

A rather rough wine, excellent if you want to forget things, such as your ......

Lindos Macro
This wine was named after Helena Lindos, the eighteenth century belle of Athens. It was she who started the now traditional smashing of plates when, one evening after her husband had drunk too much, she lost her temper and threw the family crockery at him.

Pireaus Plonkos
A strong white wine favoured by the Greek fishermen, it is said to give them courage not only when going to sea but to return to their wives. I personally tried it; and after one hour on the River Thames, I was delighted to return to my bachelor flat.

Red

Corfu Christofolilis
Not only is the name of this cheeky little wine difficult to pronounce, the wine itself is difficult to drink as it can only be obtained in goat skins. Traditionally, it must be squeezed into the mouth from a distance of one metre.

Macro Acropolis
Here is a red that is sold only after it has reached maturity. After three glasses, I found myself, rather like the building it is named after: inclined to fall down.

HUNGARY

If you've tried Bull's Blood and survived the course, I think you might enjoy some of the following, though they are rarely available outside Budapest.

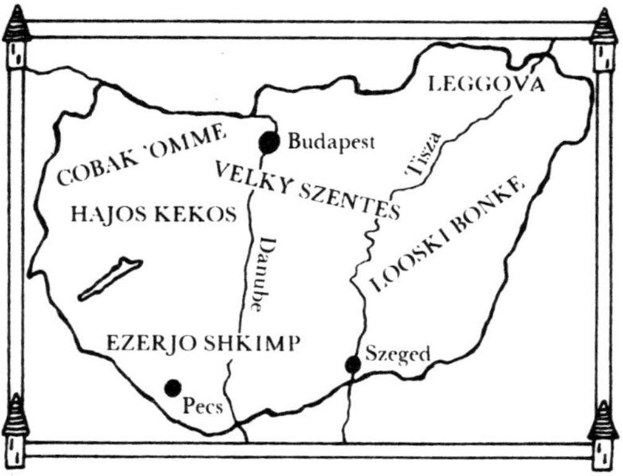

White

Looski Bonke

It is amazing how this has become so popular with teenagers in the West. I understand the Hungarian teenagers are beginning to enjoy it as well. 'Let's go and have a good old Bonke,' you'll hear them cry on a Saturday night.

Hajos Kekos

It has a charming bouquet and is nothing like the wine made in the next village, which is more like Ezerjo Shkimp.

Velky Szentes

Produced at a large vineyard on the outskirts of Budapest, this wine comes in red, white and green. Spill all three on a white tablecloth, and you have the national flag of somewhere in Africa.

Red

Cobak 'omme

After one glass, this is exactly what you will feel like doing.

Ezerjo Shkimp

Similar to the wine that is made in the next village.

Leggova

Excellent. Can't get enough of it.

USSR

The Soviet Union is now exporting more of its wines than ever before – red and white. Most but not all of those listed here are worth seeking out.

White

Gumm

This is an exciting, wicked white from the Nesski region of Mongolia, and is marketed by the famous Moscow department store. After just a few glasses of this fun-packed fluid, the only word you are likely to utter is its name.

Mukki Ural

I could not agree more.

Gorox Veena

Made from peas, this wine is surprisingly good value, and very popular with the Moscow train drivers.

Siklika
To be honest, I know nothing of this wine as I didn't test it. The name put me off completely.

Volga Veena
To translate, this means 'wine from the Volga'. (If you would like to know more, I give private lessons during the summer months.) The wine? It is white, and the name speaks for itself.

Red

Lodzvin
Very good. At least, I think it was. Or perhaps I am getting it confused with the following one.

Mazel Kosha
A lovely crisp and fruity wine. The production was first started by Chaim Cohen in 1929. But he moved on to live in California in 1936 to produce it there. He also produced twelve children and passed away peacefully in 1970.

Veska
Very red but with a hint of strength in the bouquet that suggests it should not be taken lightly. An ideal wine for a party – the Communist Party, in particular.

USA

California, more than any other state, is ideal for grape-growing due to the fine weather and San Francisco smog. Here are some interesting vintages.

White

Chateau Rosenbloom

This comes from the Pierre Rosenbloom grape, and has a milky appearance. It should not be drunk with a meat meal.

Gold Label Supreme '84

It is definitely *not* supreme and the label is white, with red print all over it.

Lily Velvet

Here is a wine from the Hollywood hills. It not only sounds like a racehorse, it tastes like one.

Villa Blanche

A youngish wine from the San Fernando Valley which, as the name suggests, is a house white.

Vine Capone

Rather too aggressive for me; popular for years at Alcatraz, though.

Vino Oyvay

Another crisp white from the Ginsberg & Cohen vineyards. Wonderful with chicken soup.

Red

American Dreame

Why they put an 'e' on the end of 'dream', I will never know. Apart from that, it is a first class white wine.

Burger White

This is a newish wine from a millionaire who once lived in Pittsburg, Pennsylvania, and made all his money in the steel business. This could explain why the wine has a sharp edge to it. Quite nice with peanuts.

Chateau Bogart

This reliable vineyard was started by Hilda Bogart soon after she arrived from Glasgow in 1907. Apart from producing fine wine, she was also the mother of that international star, Cyril Bogart.

Chateau Lincoln

A rich, red wine and typically American, in that it is normally served with ice.

Louis – Louis

An acidic red which has a tendency to repeat on you.

Pasedena Gold

If you enjoy a good red that has flavour and bouquet, this is for you. At five hundred dollars a case, I advise you to stock up.

Rosé

Vino Vegas

You would have to be a real gambler to drink this. It has a pink appearance, rather like certain ladies who walk their poodles in the car. Avoid it like the plague. Come to think of it, if you drink this, you might *catch* the plague.

AUSTRALIA

To discover the subtleties of Australian wines, you should really go to Sydney. But as he's often so busy, it's down to me. Here are a few you may like to try and some you may prefer to avoid.

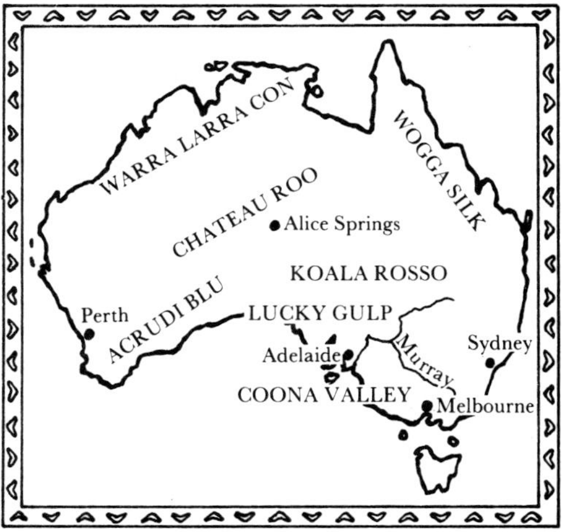

White

Acrudi Blu

A strange little wine, somewhat like a poor Chablis. Whereas most wines should be allowed to breathe, this one should be allowed to suffocate.

Chateau Roo

An excellent dry white, produced at the Kanger vineyard.

Coona Valley

One of the better wines to come from Central Victoria, it is a fine mature white, named after Sheila Coona, a renowned Melbourne nightclub singer. Full-bodied, and goes with anything.

Lucky Gulp

Here is a very unusual white that goes better with meat than with fish. Mind you, it's terrible with sandwiches.

Wogga Silk

This wine is quite difficult to come by, but worth looking for. Last week, I was lucky enough to find a bar that had a glass. Usually, by Saturday night, they have all been broken in a fight.

Red

Koala Rosso

Pleasant (if you happen to be in the outback, stuck up a eucalyptus tree, that is.)

Nolly Red

A strange acidic wine, far too red to be made from a natural grape.

Warra Larra Con

For what it is and what it costs, it is exactly what it says it is.

UNITED KINGDOM

It was a chap called Hagar Vlion, a Viking, who first introduced wine-making to the inhabitants of Britain in 1164, at a town just north of Bogsworth on the A1.

Some English wines are now quite well known, such as Nooky Fel and Tamathonk table-wine. But there are others that have yet to find their feet. (As soon as I have found mine, I shall list them for you.)

White

Bay of Belfast

Not a good wine and not a good name either, considering it is produced in the Bay of Galway. But no one seems to notice once they have drunk it. (Mind you, they don't really notice *anything* after drinking this fire water.)

Chateau Fulham '74

Not as good as the '78, but much better than the '87.

Chateau Grimsby

Not a favourite of mine, to be perfectly honest. I can't put my finger on it, but there is definitely something fishy about its taste.

Chateau Neuf du Peat

This down-to-earth wine from Cork should be opened prior to consumption and allowed to breathe for a few moments over a warm bog fire.

Ryde Lava

Sadly, this is rather disappointing. The grape suffers from sand-bite, a rare disease known only in the Ryde area. This is due to the wind blowing anti-clockwise in April and May of each leap year.

Red

Newbury Fino
As the name suggests, this is made entirely from the fino berry grape, found only around the outskirts of Teignmouth in Devon. Delicious in red or any other colour.

Paddy Tralee
You don't hear much about this Irish wine, so I won't spoil the tradition (though I will whisper that it is jolly good at a wake).

Sporran Awa
This comes from the illegal McDonald vat, operational prior to a police raid in 1986. Not easily obtainable.

Ventnor Crème
This famous Isle of White wine owes its greatness to the fact that the vineyard is sheltered by the Cowes volcano. It last erupted in 1865 but has been fairly stable since then.

Villa Mablethorpe
The French are very jealous of this super little wine. Made from a grape which grows only at Luton Airport, you really can't go wrong with this one. Duty-free, it works out at only 95p per litre.

Here's to champagne, the drink divine
That makes us forget our troubles.
It's made of a dollar's worth of wine,
And three dollars' worth of bubbles.

Anon.

SPIRITS, LIQUEURS AND CHAMPAGNE

WHISKEY

No matter how you spell it, whisk(e)y is one of the most popular spirits this side of Heaven. The Scots claim that they discovered it, as do the Irish and Welsh. They are all wrong, of course.

Whickey – I mean whisky (funny how one glass of the good stuff can have that effect on a chap) – was discovered in 1402 by Sabu Raj Smallpiece who lived in the Poona region of India. It appears he was walking, with a bag of barley, from Calcutta to the Punjab. Along the way, his curiosity got the better of him, as he wondered what would happen if the barley grains were to be heated up in water. The rest is history. But it is remarkable that the only people to find the lad wandering in a drunken stupor were three deserters from the Indian army. One was Irish, one Scottish and the other, a fellow from Liverpool. Envying the lad his condition, they forced the secret from him and couldn't wait to get home and sell the liquid to their countrymen. Upon returning, each claimed that the formula was his, and the resulting feud has continued ever since. The Welsh got to hear of it and first made their own unique blend in 1407. The Japanese have followed suit.

Irish

Kilkenny Casket

Once you have sampled this 10-year-old mixture of malts from all over the world, you will understand why it killed Kenny. (If I were his family, I would definitely sue.)

Limerich Hayes

After a few glasses of this delightful blended malt, you can't remember a single limerick because your brain's in such a haze, so you soon realise how apt the name is.

Japanese

Seeyujimmi

This is an excellent copy of the famous Scotch of the same name from Glasgow. It will cost you around 22400 yen for a litre bottle, unless you are unable to find a stockist. In this case, it will cost you a lot less.

Blended Arhso

From the Nagasoomi distillery near Kagoshowmi, this is a very informative whisky. One swig and you realise why the Japanese say 'Ah-so' so often. As it hits your throat, you give out a loud 'Aah', followed by a more painful 'So'. Then, thankfully, you pass out.

Scotch

Bally Kintyre

A blend of both Irish and Scotch malt, it has the effect of making you want to sing 'Danny Boy' in a kilt. Make sure you have a friend with you before you drink this. (It's always nice to know if you enjoyed the party, after you wake in the morning.)

Bonnie Wee Donald

First blended by a short, handsome man who lived by the River Wee, near Mushgoonoo. Different.

Welsh

Llanfanllan

Not easy to say, in any condition, this single malt comes from the LlanPew distillery in Monmouthshire. It has a taste that is rather like the one you acquire from licking a postage stamp. Passable if you drown it in ginger ale.

12-year-old Morag

Produced at the Llanfiddy distillery, it owes its unusual flavour to the water from the nearby Twynith reservoir. Just why the water should taste so distinctive remains a closely guarded secret.

GIN

Here are some gins from around the world. Rather than shaken or stirred, they are best swilled.

Addictus
This is a rare and dry gin from Athens, which I understand workmen drank while building the Acropolis. No wonder so much of it fell down.

Kremgin
A pure Russian brew produced by only the finest peasants, it is made from left-over Vodka grain, which is swept up and re-boiled. A little *eau de cologne* is added to give just the right flavour.

Silver Balkan
If you live in the Balkans, you will know how popular this gin is.

Trilby Gin
Here is a fine dry gin from a Hatfield distillery, and ideal for mixing with tonic water or lemon juice. It was discovered in the German city of Homburg. The man who first drank it neat went as mad as a hatter.

Virgin Gin
Regrettably, I cannot comment on this label since, candidly, no one has been able to try it as yet.

BRANDY

I suppose *you* think of the French when you think of brandy. I always think of the late Betty Huxley-Bore. (Not that she has left this world. It's just that after six large cognacs, she always forgets where and when her next appointment is.) But I digress. Here are some brandies that may be new to you.

Bella Nuneaton

This unusual Armagnac is made by the 'Preserve Britain' group who insist that, within ten years, the coastline will have been eroded by up to two hundred miles. It is produced at Coventry-on-Sea.

Brandiski Glasnost

A great brandy for turning strangers into friends. After a bottle of this delightful brew, your eyes become the same colour as the Russian flag.

Brando

From the famous house of Marlon, this American brandy is pure luxury. Three glasses and you will be walking on six inch pile carpet.

Brandy Lookyu

This brandy is made by the Davies family at Llandeveilinme, Wales, and is boiled for a period of five hours in a miner's tin bath.

Cyrano de Bercognac

You really do need a good nose to enjoy such a fine French brandy.

Honalulu Kahzi

Known locally in Hawaii as 'Umm' because of the warm, comforting feeling you get in the stomach as it slides gently down to its destination, it is a must after a ten course meal.

Mealendo Fin

A perfect brandy that goes down well at the end of dinner, it originates in Finland. It is not recommended at the end of lunch, though. (A few at that time of the day and *you* could be the one going down.)

Velvet Haggis

Not as smooth as the name suggests, this brandy is, nevertheless, a fine example of what can be done within the confines of McAuchtey prison. The exotic burnt flavour comes from the boiling of the liquid in a kilt, lined with tin-foil. This is a slow process, but time is on the inmates' side.

LIQUEURS

Many people, myself included, are rather partial to a fine liqueur at the end of a meal. In fact, some people, myself most definitely included, enjoy a good liqueur *before* a meal, especially before breakfast.

Here are a few lesser-known liqueurs that I have stumbled across.

Belladonna Original
An excellent gift for your bank manager, when he refuses to give you that much needed overdraft.

Crème de Cacow
Whoever it was that said this was worth stocking up with was talking a lot of bull, I'd say.

Drambluie
Created by an elderly Scottish lady and her Australian husband, this is a liqueur you can really savour. Ladies have to be careful not to spill it over their fingers, though, as it will remove varnish.

Fredbuca
This delightful liqueur is also from the Sambuca family, and is similar to that warming white liquid except for the burning of coffee beans. With Fredbuca, you burn tea-bags.

SHERRY

Many countries have tried to copy the great Spanish sherries: but these have failed, in my humble opinion, to come up to the originals. Serve any of the following as an aperitif, and enjoy the look of surprise over your guests' faces.

Coops
Pronounced 'Cock-ups', this sherry is from the Epsom stable.

Hardy's Bradford Cream
This comes in three different colours, and a bottle.

Sandewoman
A medium dry sherry with a feminine bouquet, it is pure delight.

Tio Pipi
This is a fine, light sherry of great distinction. It was awarded the Silver Cork at last year's Irish beer festival.

Toro Pazo
This Spanish delight is a must for all collectors of rare sherry. It is almost impossible to find anywhere.

Triple Century
A medium cream of great tradition. Poured into a dish of goulash, it will keep you going for hours.

CHAMPAGNE

There was a time when only the very rich could afford this delightful drink. Now, it seems, almost anyone can buy it. Napoleon drank gallons of it, I am told; and what was good enough for him is good enough for me. Here are some new champagnes that you might like.

Billinger
This is not to be confused with the American gangster of the same name. On the contrary, it is more likely to hold you down than hold you up.

Dadd & Co
Not as good as Mumm but every bit as sparkling.

Don Perrynon
This is simply delightful, if you can afford it. If you can't, then I suggest that you buy something cheaper.

Mote & Shandon
This popular choice of champers is almost as good as the other one from the same region, but not quite.

Verve Cliquough
Smooth and creamy with lots of beautiful bubbles to tickle your nose, this is a must for your cellar. It is also quite nice in the dining room.

GLOSSARY

Appellation Controllée
A French wine inspection to make sure that no apple juice has been added.

Body
No wine drinker should be without one.

Bouquet
A fragrance that can vary somewhat. It all depends on the feet that trod the grapes.

Chambré
A store room for champagne before it matures.

Corked
Irish slang for being intoxicated.

Fortified
The condition a drinker believes he is in, just before he falls over.

Fruitiness
A pleasant feeling brought on by alcohol.

Heady
The region of a wine bottle that is just above the necky.

Nose
Heavy drinkers have large ones that turn red when they have had sufficient.

Oxidized
The feeling the tongue develops after a night on cheap vino.